Contents

Gran's birthday

Gran had a picnic for her 60th birthday party.

Everyone enjoyed themselves.

Gran had a cake with candles on it.
Kirsty and Lewis helped her blow them out.

Kirsty likes to see what Gran was like when she was a little girl.

This is an older photograph of Gran. How can you tell?

Do you think it looks like Gran?

Grandpa works on a farm. He likes driving his tractor.

When Grandpa was a boy his father drove a tractor like this. How is it different?

This is one of Grandpa's oldest photographs, taken about 60 years ago.

It is his Grandpa.
He worked on a farm.
Why do you think he needed horses?

Gran goes to school

Gran lived by the sea
when she was little.

She had to walk to school.
Sometimes it was dark.

At the weekend, Gran used
to watch the fishermen
in their boats.

This modern photograph was taken at the same place.

Gran still likes to see the boats in the harbour.

Are the ships the same?
What is different?

Lewis enjoys playing with his friends at school. Football is his favourite game.

Sometimes Grandpa takes Lewis to see a football match.

Grandpa has supported the same team for 50 years.

Do you like football?

Kirsty and Lewis help Gran with her shopping. Sometimes they get a treat.

When Gran was little a van came to her house selling groceries. Sometimes she had to queue.

Grandpa's vegetables

Gran's Dad grew all his own vegetables.

Grandpa still likes to grow vegetables. He grows carrots, potatoes, leeks, turnips, peas and cabbages, just like his own Dad did.

Gran makes broth with Grandpa's vegetables, from a recipe her Gran gave her.

200g neck of lamb
25g pearl barley
50g dried peas
1 each large carrot, onion, leek, chopped
1 small turnip, chopped
50g shredded cabbage
Salt and pepper

Put meat into 2 pints of water with salt and pepper, barley and peas. Simmer for 1 hour. Add chopped vegetables and simmer for 30 minutes. Add cabbage and simmer for 15 minutes. Season and serve.

On Grandpa's 8th birthday, 50 years ago, he got this birthday postcard from his grandparents.

Many Glad Wishes for your 8th Birthday.

To mark the date Now you are Eight, Please take this card of mine, With wishes true That all for you, A lucky star may shine.

At the 'pictures'

As a special treat, his Mum and Dad took him to the 'pictures' and out to afternoon tea.

He can remember falling asleep on the bus on the way home.

Have you had a birthday treat?
Did you go on a bus?

This is Gran and Grandpa getting married 35 years ago.

Mum and Dad's wedding

Kirsty and Lewis's Mum and Dad had a ceilidh for their wedding.

Gran kept a 'favour' from the wedding cake and gave it to Kirsty.

Kirsty thinks the dancing looks fun.

Have you been to a wedding like this?

Three generations

This photograph was taken 30 years ago. Grandpa is holding Kirsty and Lewis's Dad when he was 10 days old.

This photograph is 7 years old. It is of Lewis.

The babies are wearing the same shawl. Gran's Mum made it for her first baby. Gran gave it to Lewis's Mum when he was born.

Index

Acknowledgements

We are grateful to the following for permission to reproduce copyright photographs:

Trevor Clifford Photography, pages 2-3 (below) 11 (below), 14 (below); Hulton Deutsch Collection, pages 4 (below, 6 (above); Topham Picturepoint, pages 10 (below), 13.
All remaining photographs were supply by the author.

We have been unable to trace the copyright holder for the photographs on pages 6-7, 12, and would be grateful for any information that would enable us to do so.

Front cover : Author

IFC : Author

Back cover : Author

Picture Research by Sandie Huskinson-Rolfe (PHOTOSEEKERS)

Grandparents in Scotland

ISBN 0-582-24848-5

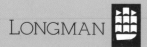

LONGMAN

9 780582 248489